Preface

Welcome to the exciting world of computers! TAP AND LEARN For Class 4 book, designed for students, is an engaging and comprehensive introduction to computer science. Our goal is to spark curiosity and provide a strong foundation in computer literacy, preparing young minds for a future where technology plays a central role. In today's world, computers are everywhere. From schools and homes to offices and shops, they have become an integral part of our lives. Understanding how computers work and how to use them effectively is crucial for success in almost every field. This book aims to make learning about computers fun and easy for young students.

This book is structured to introduce students gradually to the world of computers, ensuring that they understand each concept thoroughly before moving on to the next. Here's a brief overview of what you will find in the chapters: We begin with the basics, answering the fundamental question: What is a computer? Students will learn about the various types of computers and their uses in different environments. This chapter introduces the physical parts of a computer. Students will learn about input devices like the keyboard and mouse, output devices like monitors and printers, and the central processing unit (CPU) which acts as the brain of the computer. Here, we explain the difference between hardware and software. Students will be introduced to system software and application software, learning how software enables hardware to perform useful tasks. Students will learn about operating systems, the essential software that manages all hardware and other software on a computer. This chapter covers basic functions and navigation tips. This chapter introduces the basic concepts of programming in a simple and engaging way. Through fun activities, students will develop logical thinking and problem-solving skills. We cover the use of common applications such as word processors and drawing programs. Students will learn to create and save documents, use basic editing tools, and enjoy creating their own art digitally. As students begin to explore the internet, it's crucial to teach them how to stay safe online. This chapter covers important tips on how to use the internet responsibly, avoid sharing personal information, and recognize potential online dangers. Proper computer care and etiquette are essential skills. Students will learn how to maintain their devices, use computers responsibly, and follow good practices to ensure a healthy and productive computing environment.

Our approach combines theoretical knowledge with practical activities to make learning enjoyable and effective. Each chapter includes illustrations and diagrams to help students visualize concepts, hands-on activities that reinforce learning, and review questions to assess understanding and retention of the

Table of Contents

Chapter 1: Data Storage and Memory

In this chapter you will learn about:

Computer Memory
Measuring the Computer's Memory

Every computer needs memory to function, just like humans need their brains to store and retrieve information. When you open a game or save a school project on a computer, it uses its memory and storage systems to help you. There are different types of memory, each with its own role in storing and processing information.

This chapter will explore how computer memory works, how it is measured, and why different storage devices are used. We will also discuss the fun world of cloud storage and introduce you to the exciting concept of measuring digital memory!

1.1 Computer Memory

Computer memory is essential for efficiently operating programs, applications, and the operating system itself. It can be divided into two types: Primary Memory and Secondary Memory. Primary memory is used when the computer is running programs, while secondary memory is where data is stored for the long term. Let's explore both types in detail.

1.1.1 Primary Memory (Volatile Memory)

Primary memory is also known as volatile memory because it works only when the computer is turned on. When the computer is switched off, the data stored in the primary memory is erased.

1.1.1.1 RAM (Random Access Memory)

RAM stores the active data and programs that the computer is currently using.
It allows the computer to access the information it needs to complete tasks quickly.
More RAM means the computer can handle more tasks simultaneously (like opening many browser tabs).
Think of RAM like a desk where you do your homework – the bigger the desk, the more books and papers you can keep while working.

1.1.1.2 Cache Memory

The cache is a small memory built inside the CPU (Central Processing Unit) or close to it.
It stores frequently used data, so the CPU doesn't have to fetch it from slower memory sources.
Cache memory makes the computer faster by reducing the time needed to access data.
Think of cache memory like sticky notes you keep handy – you quickly grab them instead of searching through your entire notebook.

1.1.2 Secondary Memory (Non-Volatile Memory)

Secondary memory stores data permanently. Even if the computer is turned off, the information remains safe. It is used for storing files, programs, and the operating system.

1.1.2.1 Hard Disk Drive (HDD)

An HDD uses spinning disks to read and write data.
It has moving parts, which makes it slower and more prone to damage than SSDs.
HDDs are usually less expensive and can store a lot of data (up to several terabytes).
It is like a school locker where you keep things safe for a long time.

1.1.2.2 Solid-State Drive (SSD)

An SSD has no moving parts and uses flash memory to store data.
It is much faster than HDDs and more durable since it doesn't have spinning disks.
SSDs are used in modern computers for faster startup and program loading.
Think of it like a magic backpack where everything appears instantly when you need it!

1.1.2.3 USB Drives and Memory Cards

USB drives are portable devices used to transfer files between computers.
Memory cards store data for devices like cameras and smartphones.
They are small, lightweight, and can store a lot of information.

1.1.2.4 Cloud Storage

Cloud storage allows users to store their files on the internet.
Services like Google Drive and Dropbox provide access to files from any device with an internet connection.
It is like a virtual cupboard you can open from anywhere in the world!

Feature	Primary Memory	Secondary Memory
Nature	Volatile (data lost when power is off)	Non-volatile (data remains even without power)
Location	Located inside the CPU or on the motherboard	Located in internal or external storage devices
Speed	Extremely fast (RAM, Cache)	Slower compared to RAM and cache (HDDs, SSDs)
Capacity	Limited capacity (typically a few GBs)	Larger capacity (up to several TBs)
Purpose	Stores active programs and data being used	Stores files, programs, and the operating system
Accessibility	Directly accessible by the CPU	It needs to be loaded into RAM for processing
Examples	RAM, Cache	HDD, SSD, USB drives, Cloud storage
Usage	Temporary data storage while tasks are running	Permanent storage for long-term use

1.2 Measuring the Computer's Memory

Computer memory is essential for storing and processing data. To understand how much information a computer can hold and handle, we use specific units to measure it. These units range from bits to terabytes. Below, we will explore these units to understand their size, real-life applications, and why they are essential.

1.2.1 Bit (Binary Digit)

A bit is the smallest unit of data in a computer.
It can hold only two values: 0 or 1 (binary system).
Think of it like a light switch: when it is OFF, it represents 0; when ON, it means 1.
A computer uses billions of bits every second to process instructions and data.

Example: A bit is used in basic digital circuits like alarm clocks, which understand only two states: active (1) and inactive (0).

1.2.2. Byte (B)

A byte consists of 8 bits.
A byte can represent a single character such as the letter 'A', a number like '5', or a symbol like '@'.
Computers store characters in bytes, so every letter you type or key you press takes up one byte.
Example: If you write the word "Hello," it takes 5 bytes because there are 5 characters.

1.2.3. Kilobyte (KB)

1 KB (Kilobyte) = 1,024 bytes.
Kilobytes are used to measure small files, such as text documents, emails, or configuration files.
Most simple text files or tiny images are measured in kilobytes.
Example: A one-page Word document without images is around 20 to 30 KB.
An SMS text message can range between 1 and 3 KB, depending on its length.

1.2.4. Megabyte (MB)

1 MB (Megabyte) = 1,024 KB.
Larger files like music, images, and short videos are often measured in megabytes.
A song in MP3 format is usually around 3 to 5 MB.
Applications on your phone or computer, such as photo-editing software, also take up several megabytes.
Example: A high-resolution photo may be around 2 to 10 MB.
A minute-long song in MP3 format takes about 4 MB of space.

1.2.5. Gigabyte (GB)

1 GB (Gigabyte) = 1,024 MB.
A gigabyte measures larger files or data collections, such as software programs, movies, and storage capacities.
Modern smartphones typically have storage capacities of 64 GB, 128 GB, or even higher to store photos, videos, apps, and more.
A high-definition (HD) movie can take up about 2 to 4 GB of space.
Example: A large game like Minecraft can be around 300 MB to 1 GB.
Smartphones with 128 GB storage can store thousands of photos and hundreds of songs.

1.2.6. Terabyte (TB)

1 TB (Terabyte) = 1,024 GB.
Terabytes are used to measure substantial storage capacities, such as the storage available in data centres, servers, or high-end computers.
Many external hard drives and modern computer systems offer 1 TB or more of storage to keep large amounts of data.
Example: A 1 TB external hard drive can store about 250 movies or more than 300,000 photos.
Servers in data centres hold several terabytes of data, helping websites, applications, and services run smoothly.

Why is Memory Measurement Important?
Understanding memory measurements helps us:
Manage device storage: Knowing how much space an app or file takes can help prevent storage from running out.
Optimize performance: Devices with more memory (like GBs of RAM) perform tasks faster.
Choose the suitable storage device: A user with many photos may need a 1 TB external drive, while someone with fewer files might need only a 64 GB USB drive.
Plan for backups: Cloud services offer different storage plans measured in GBs or TBs, helping users decide their needs.

1.3 Glossary

Memory: Temporary storage used by a computer to run programs.
USB Drive: A portable storage device used to transfer data.
Cloud Storage: Internet-based storage accessible from any device.
Bit: The smallest data unit in a computer, representing a 0 or 1.
Byte: A unit of data made up of 8 bits.
Kilobyte (KB): A unit of memory equal to 1,024 bytes.
Gigabyte (GB): A unit of memory equal to 1,024 megabytes.

1.4 Summary

Computer memory is essential for running programs and storing data efficiently.
Memory is divided into primary memory (RAM, Cache) and secondary memory (HDD, SSD, USB).
RAM is a volatile memory that holds data temporarily, while secondary memory stores data permanently.
Cache memory speeds up processes by storing frequently used data close to the CPU.
Storage devices include HDDs, SSDs, memory cards, USB drives, and cloud storage.
Cloud storage allows access to files from any device with an internet connection.
Computer memory is measured in bits, bytes, kilobytes, megabytes, gigabytes, and terabytes.

Exercise

Exercise 1 – Choose the Correct Answer
1. Which type of memory stores data temporarily and is erased when the computer is turned off?
a) Hard Disk Drive
b) Cloud Storage
c) RAM
d) USB Drive
2. What unit is used to measure very large storage capacities, like those in hard drives?

a) Kilobyte
b) Megabyte
c) Gigabyte
d) Terabyte

Exercise 2 – True/False
1. Cache memory is a type of secondary memory.
2. A bit is the smallest unit of data in a computer.

Exercise 3 – Rearrange the Sentence
1. computer is important memory for the
2. used storing data permanently Secondary memory is for

Exercise 4 – Choose the Odd One Out
1. a) RAM b) SSD c) USB Drive d) Cache
2. a) Bit b) Byte c) Kilobyte d) Cache

Exercise 5 – Short Questions
1. What is the difference between RAM and HDD?
2. Why is cache memory important for a computer?

Answer

Exercise 1- 1. c) RAM, 2. d) Terabyte
Exercise 2- 1. False, 2. d) True
Exercise 3- 1. Memory is important for the computer.
2. Secondary memory is used for storing data permanently.
Exercise 4- 1. b,2. d.

Project

Explore different types of storage devices and their uses.

Activity

Explore the difference between primary and secondary memory.

Case Study

Riya is working on a school project that involves creating a slideshow with pictures, a video presentation, and a few text documents. She wants to save her project in a way that she can work on it from both home and school, and she needs to share it with her teacher.

Questions for Students:

What type of storage should Riya use to make her project accessible from both home and school? (Hint: Think about cloud storage or USB drives.)

Why might cloud storage be a good choice for Riya's project?

If Riya had only large media files and no internet, which type of storage would be most convenient for her?

Group Discussion

Discuss to think critically about the role of memory in computers and to practice expressing their thoughts in a group setting.

Chapter-1
TEST PAPER
Data Storage and Memory

Time Duration: 20 Minutes **Maximum Marks: 10**

General Instructions:

1. The question paper consists of 10 questions.
2. All questions are compulsory.

True/False- **(1 X 2 = 2 marks)**

1. RAM is a type of secondary memory.
2. A byte is made up of 8 bits.

Choose the Correct Option **(1 X 3 = 3 marks)**

1. Which memory is temporary and is erased when the computer is turned off?
a) HDD
b) USB Drive
c) RAM
d) SSD
2. Which unit of measurement is the largest?
a) Kilobyte
b) Megabyte
c) Gigabyte
d) Terabyte
3. Which of these is a portable storage device?
a) Cache
b) RAM
c) USB Drive
d) Cloud Storage

Short Questions **(1 X 5 = 5 marks)**

1. What is the difference between primary and secondary memory?
2. Give one example of primary memory and one example of secondary memory.
3. Why is cache memory important for a computer?
4. What is a byte, and how many bits make up a byte?
5. Name a storage device that allows you to save files online and access them from anywhere.

Online Interactive Resources

Online Exam Paper:
Link: https://forms.gle/FnELis5cHL5HR56W9

QR Code:

Chapter 1 Videos Playlist:
Link: https://www.youtube.com/playlist?list=PLzlh_31VWEFoNHd55iUh3N03TP_jPTTaa

QR Code:

Chapter 2: Managing Files and Folder

In this chapter, you will learn about:

- Features of Windows 11
- Creating a folder
- Right-clicking a Folder
- Shortcuts
- Creating a file
- Right-clicking a File
- Desktop of Windows
- Task View

In today's digital world, learning to manage files and folders is essential. Windows 11, the latest operating system from Microsoft, offers many new features to help users keep their digital work organized, whether for school projects, photos, or games. Just like we keep our schoolbooks and notebooks neatly arranged in our bags or on shelves, files and folders on a computer need to be stored properly to make it easier to find and use them later.

This chapter introduces the basics of working with files (where information is saved) and folders (containers used to store files). It also covers new features in Windows 11 that make working on computers more enjoyable and efficient. Students will learn how to create and rename files and folders, use shortcuts, and explore the Windows desktop and taskbar. Another exciting feature of Windows 11 is the Task View, which makes multitasking easy by showing all open apps and windows at a glance. With this, students can organise their activities across multiple desktops—just like having a different notebook for each subject!

Managing files and folders on a computer is not just a skill for school but a lifelong skill. As students grow, they will deal with more digital data—whether for higher studies, work, or hobbies—and knowing how to keep this data organized will be invaluable. Understanding these concepts now will prepare students to confidently use computers, not only for learning but also for personal and future professional use.

2.1 Features of Windows 11

Windows 11 offers a lot of improvements over older versions, making it more efficient and visually appealing.

Start Menu: New, centered Start menu with quick access to apps and files.
Widgets Panel: Displays news, weather, calendar events, and reminders.
Rounded Corners and Smooth Animations: A cleaner design with soft, rounded corners.
Snap Layouts: Helps arrange multiple windows neatly for multitasking.
Virtual Desktops: Allows users to create multiple desktops for different purposes.
Taskbar Improvements: Centralized taskbar with quick access to apps.
Touchscreen Compatibility: Optimized for touchscreen devices.
Fast Search: Find files, apps, and settings easily using the Search option.
Fun Fact: Windows 11 allows you to use voice typing! Just press the Windows + H keys to start speaking instead of typing.

2.2 Creating a file

A file is where information or data is stored on a computer. Files can be documents, pictures, videos, or programs. Creating a file is the first step to saving and organising your work.

Steps to Create a File:
Right-click on the desktop or inside a folder.
Click New from the menu.
Select the type of file you want to create (e.g., Word document or Text file).
Name the file and press Enter.
Fun Fact: You can quickly rename a file by clicking it once and pressing the F2 key!

2.3 Creating a folder

A folder is a digital container where files can be stored. Organising files in folders makes them easy to find.

Steps to Create a Folder:
Right-click on the desktop or inside a folder.
Choose New and then click Folder.
Name the folder and press Enter.
Fun Fact: You can nest folders inside other folders. It's like having folders within folders, just like books inside a bookshelf!

2.4 Right-clicking a File

When you right-click a file, a menu with several useful options appears.

Options Available When Right-Clicking a File:
Open: Open the file.
Copy/Paste: Make copies of the file.
Rename: Change the file's name.
Delete: Remove the file.
Properties: View the file's size and details.
Fun Fact: Did you accidentally delete a file? Don't worry! Files go to the Recycle Bin, from where you can restore them.

2.5 Right-clicking a Folder

Right-clicking on a folder provides similar options to those available for files, with some additional features.

Options Available When Right-Clicking a Folder:
Open: View the contents of the folder.
Copy/Paste: Duplicate the folder.
Rename: Give the folder a new name.
Properties: See details like size and number of items.
Send to: Move or send the folder to a different location or external drive.
Fun Fact: You can use Ctrl + Z to undo any accidental deletions or movements of folders!

2.6 Desktop of Windows

The desktop is the first screen you see after logging in. It holds icons, shortcuts, and the taskbar. Think of it like your desk in school, where you keep important things within easy reach.

Desktop Features:
Icons: Small images that represent files, folders, or applications.
Taskbar: A strip at the bottom of the screen showing open programs and the Start menu.
Widgets: Information panels like weather, calendar, and to-do lists.
Fun Fact: You can move icons around on the desktop by clicking and dragging them!

2.7 Shortcuts

A shortcut is a quick way to open a file, folder, or application. Its icons have small arrows.

How to Create a Shortcut:
Right-click on a file, folder, or app.
Select Create Shortcut.
Drag the shortcut to the desktop or a folder.
Fun Fact: Did you know that pressing Alt + Tab instantly lets you switch between open windows?

2.8 Task View

- ✓ Task View is a feature that lets you see all the open apps and desktops. It's helpful for multitasking.

Using Task View:
Click the Task View button on the taskbar (two overlapping squares).
See all the open apps and switch between them.
Create new desktops for different activities, such as one for homework and one for games.
Fun Fact: You can quickly open Task View by pressing Windows + Tab!

2.9 Glossary

File: A collection of data stored on a computer.
Folder: A virtual container for organising files.
Shortcut: A quick link to open files, folders, or applications.
Task View: A feature that shows all open windows and desktops.
Desktop: The primary screen where files, folders, and shortcuts are placed.
Taskbar: A bar at the bottom of the screen that shows open apps and quick access tools.
Recycle Bin: A place where deleted files are stored temporarily.
Properties: Information about a file or folder.

2.10 Summary

Windows 11 is the latest operating system with new features like Snap Layouts, Widgets, and Virtual Desktops.
Files are used to store data, and folders help organise them.
Right-clicking on files or folders gives you options like Open, Rename, or Delete.
The desktop is where you keep your most used files and apps.
Shortcuts provide quick access to files, apps, or folders.
Task View helps manage open apps and desktops for better multitasking.

Exercise

Exercise 1 – Choose the Correct Answer

1. Which feature in Windows 11 allows you to arrange open windows neatly for multitasking?
a) Widgets
b) Snap Layouts
c) Task View
d) Recycle Bin
2. What does the Task View feature in Windows 11 allow you to do?
a) Delete files
b) View all open windows and desktops
c) Create shortcuts
d) Access the Recycle Bin

Exercise 2 – True/False

1. Right-clicking on a file in Windows 11 gives you options like Open, Rename, and Delete.
2. The Task View feature recovers deleted files in Windows 11.

Exercise 3 – Choose the Odd One Out

1. Which one of these is not a feature of Windows 11?
a) Snap Layouts
b) Task View
c) Recycle Bin
d) Document Scanner
2. Choose the option that is not related to file management.
a) Task View
b) Desktop
c) Widgets
d) Properties

Exercise 4 – Match Case

COLUMN A	COLUMN B
a) Snap Layouts	i) Provides options like Rename or Delete
b) Recycle Bin	ii) Arranges open windows neatly
c) Right-clicking a file	iii) Organizes multiple files
d) Creating a folder	iv) Stores deleted files temporarily

Exercise 5 – Short Questions

1. What is the purpose of the Recycle Bin in Windows 11?
2. How does Task View help multitask on Windows 11?

Answer

Exercise 1- 1.b) Snap Layouts, 2.b) View all open windows and desktops
Exercise 2- 1.True, 2.False
Exercise 3- 1.d) Document Scanner, 2.c) Widgets
Exercise 4- a-ii, b-iv, c-i, d- iii.

Project

Explore how to organize files and folders on a computer effectively.

Activity

Practice finding and managing files and folders with a fun scavenger hunt game.

Case Study

Maya is a fourth-grade student who loves creating digital artwork and saving interesting articles. Over time, her desktop has become cluttered with files named things like "Untitled1," "Image123," and "Doc (2)." Maya often wastes time trying to find the right file.

Discussion Questions:
How would you help Maya organise her desktop so she can find her files faster?
What would be a good system to use if you were Maya, with so many creative projects

Group Discussion

Discuss the importance of digital organisation and managing files and folders.

Chapter-2
TEST PAPER
Managing Files and Folder

Time Duration: 20 Minutes **Maximum Marks: 10**

General Instructions:

1. The question paper consists of 10 questions.
2. All questions are compulsory.

True/False **(1 x 2 = 2 marks)**

1. The Recycle Bin in Windows 11 permanently deletes files immediately.
2. Right-clicking a folder gives you options to rename and delete it.

Choose the Correct Option **(1 x 3 = 3 marks)**

1. Which feature in Windows 11 allows you to arrange open windows?
a) Widgets
b) Snap Layouts
c) Taskbar
d) Task View
2. What is the primary use of the Task View feature?
a) Organizing files into folders
b) Viewing all open windows and desktops
c) Searching for files
d) Renaming files
3. Which option is not available when you right-click a file?
a) Open
b) Copy
c) Resize
d) Delete

Short Questions **(1 x 5 = 5 marks)**

1. Define the purpose of a folder on a computer.
2. How does creating shortcuts help in managing files?
3. What happens to a file when it is deleted from a folder?
4. Explain the function of the Taskbar in Windows 11.
5. Why is organizing files and folders important on a computer?

Online Interactive Resources

Online Exam Paper:
Link: https://forms.gle/JBHhYNE3ct1J4Wr86

QR Code:

Chapter 2 Videos Playlist:

Link: https://www.youtube.com/playlist?list=PLzlh_31VWEFqa4fjaMHB5CZRChqho7NSV

QR Code:

Chapter 3: Create Magic with PowerPoint

In this chapter you will learn about:

Starting PowerPoint
Adding a New Slide
Adding Picture to a Slide
Saving a Presentation
Exiting from PowerPoint
Editing SmartArt
Using Action Buttons
Interface of PowerPoint
Changing the Layout of a Slide
Viewing Slides in Different Views
Opening a Saved Presentation
Inserting SmartArt on a Slide
Inserting Audio Clips
Printing Presentation

PowerPoint is a popular software developed by Microsoft that helps people create presentations. A presentation is like a slideshow with text, pictures, animations, and sounds. PowerPoint makes it easy to share ideas and tell stories creatively! PowerPoint is a fun and helpful tool, whether you're giving a class presentation or making a birthday slideshow. Let's explore step by step how you can create magic with PowerPoint!

3.1 Starting PowerPoint

To start PowerPoint:
Open Microsoft PowerPoint from the Start Menu on your computer.
Click on Blank Presentation to create a new presentation.
If you have an existing presentation, click Open and choose the file you want.

3.2 Interface of PowerPoint

The interface includes:
Title Bar: Displays the name of your presentation.
Ribbon: Contains tabs with tools and options like Home, Insert, and Design.
Slides Pane: Shows all the slides in your presentation on the left side.
Slide Area: Displays the current slide you are working on.
Notes Section: Allows you to add notes for each slide.
Quick Access Toolbar: Offers shortcuts for Save, Undo, Redo, and more.
View Options: At the bottom, you can switch views, like Normal and Slide Sorter.

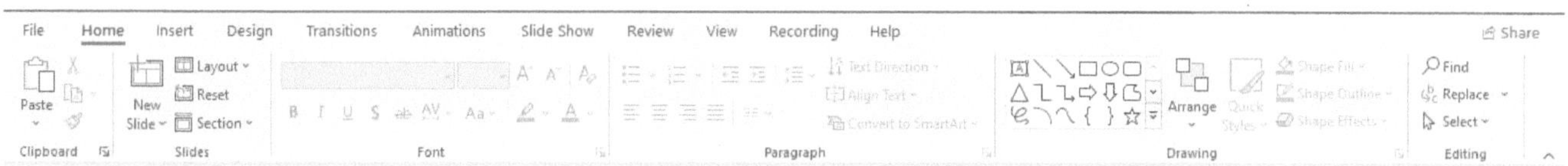

3.3 Adding a New Slide

You can't create a presentation without slides! To add a new slide:
Go to the Home tab and click "New Slide".
Choose the layout that best fits your content (like a Title Slide or Content Slide).
Right-click on the slide pane and select "New Slide".
Fun Fact:
The first presentation slide is usually called the Title Slide because it introduces the topic.

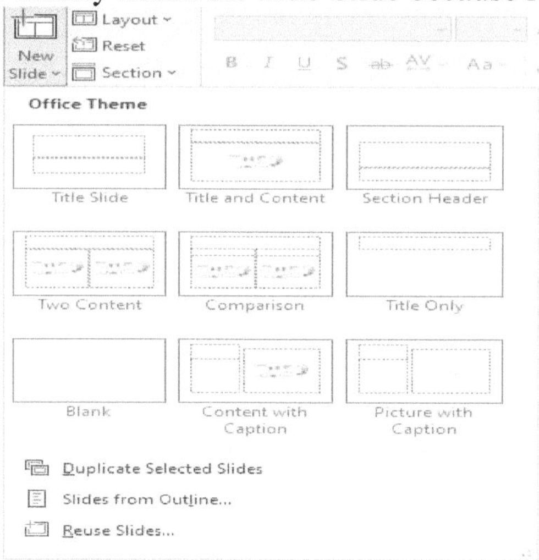

3.4 Changing the Layout of a Slide

Sometimes, the layout of a slide needs to change based on the type of information you want to present.
Click on the slide you want to change.
Go to the Home tab → Layout.
Choose from Title and Content, Two Content, or Blank Slide.
Fun Fact:
A well-chosen layout helps your audience understand your message better!

3.5 Adding Picture to a Slide

Pictures make your presentation more exciting! To add a picture:
Click on the Insert tab → Pictures.
Select "This Device" to upload a picture from your computer, or choose "Online Pictures" to find one online.
Resize the picture by dragging the corners and moving it around as needed.
Fun Fact:
You can also use animated GIFs to make your slides look lively and fun!

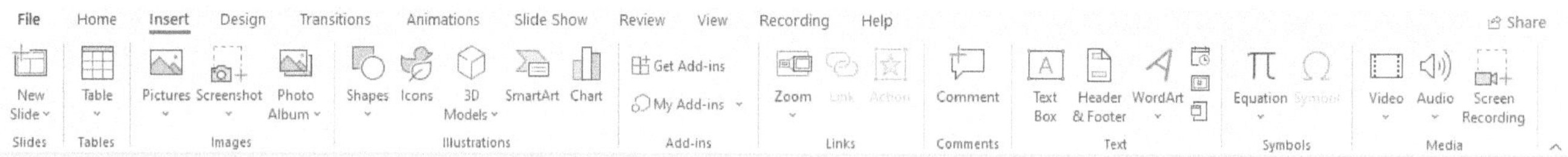

3.6 Viewing Slides in Different Views

PowerPoint offers different views to help you organise your slides effectively.
Normal View: Edit one slide at a time.
Slide Sorter: See all slides at once as small thumbnails.
Reading View: View the slides without animations or transitions.
Slide Show: Play the presentation in full-screen mode.
Fun Fact:
Slide Sorter view is perfect for quickly rearranging the order of slides!

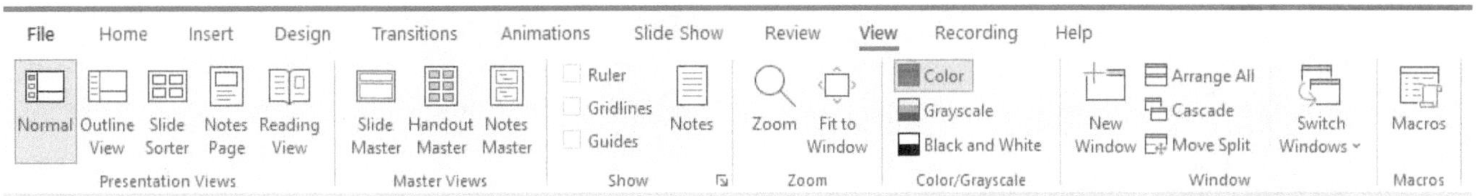

3.7 Saving a Presentation

To avoid losing your hard work, remember to save your presentation!
Click File → Save As.
Choose a location on your computer, like Desktop or Documents.
Give your presentation a name and click Save.
Fun Fact:
PowerPoint has an AutoSave feature that can save your work every few minutes!

3.8 Opening a Saved Presentation

To continue working on a saved presentation:
Click File → Open.
Browse your computer for the saved file.
Select the file and click Open.
Fun Fact:
You can open PowerPoint files on Google Slides too!

3.9 Exiting from PowerPoint

To close PowerPoint:
Click File → Exit.
Or, click the X button at the top-right corner of the window.
If you have unsaved changes, PowerPoint will ask if you want to save before exiting.
Fun Fact:
Pressing Alt + F4 on your keyboard is a shortcut to exit any program, including PowerPoint.

3.10 Inserting SmartArt on a Slide

SmartArt helps you display ideas visually.
Click the Insert tab → SmartArt.
Choose a type, like Process, Hierarchy, or Cycle.

Add your text inside the boxes.
Fun Fact:
SmartArt diagrams automatically resize to fit your text, so your presentation always looks neat!

3.11 Editing SmartArt

You can modify SmartArt to make it more engaging:
Click on the SmartArt to select it.
Use the SmartArt Tools to change colors and styles.
Add or remove boxes by clicking Add Shape or Remove Shape.
Fun Fact:
SmartArt animations make diagrams come alive during a presentation!

3.12 Inserting Audio Clips

You can add sounds to make your slides more interesting.
Click on the Insert tab → Audio.
Choose Audio on My PC or Record Audio to insert a clip.
You can set the audio to play Automatically or When Clicked.
Fun Fact:
You can play background music across all your slides using PowerPoint's audio tools.

3.13 Using Action Buttons

Action buttons are interactive buttons you can click to navigate through slides.
Click on the Insert tab → Shapes.
Choose an Action Button like Home or Play.
Link it to another slide or set it to play a sound.
Fun Fact:
You can create quizzes using Action Buttons to make learning fun!

3.14 Printing Presentation

Sometimes, you may need to print your slides for sharing.
Click File → Print.
Choose the printer and the number of slides per page.
Click Print to get a hard copy of your presentation.
Fun Fact:
You can print your slides as handouts with space for notes beside each slide!

3.15 Glossary

Slide: A single page in a presentation.
Presentation: A collection of slides.
SmartArt: A diagram that presents ideas visually.
Layout: The way text and content are arranged on a slide.

Ribbon: The toolbar with all the tools and commands.
Action Button: A clickable button to navigate or perform tasks.
Slide Sorter: A view showing all slides as small thumbnails.
Audio Clip: A sound file added to a slide.
AutoSave: A feature that saves your presentation automatically.
Thumbnail: A small version of a slide used for previews.

3.16 Summary

Understand the different parts of the PowerPoint window.
Add new slides to your presentation.
Change slide layouts to organise content more effectively.
Insert images to make your slides more engaging.
Use different views such as Normal, Slide Sorter, and Slide Show for various tasks.
Save your work regularly to prevent losing progress.
Open saved presentations to continue working on them.
Close the program safely after completing your presentation.
Use SmartArt diagrams to display information visually.
Modify SmartArt to suit your presentation needs better.
Add sounds to slides to make them more attractive.
Use action buttons to create interactive presentations.
Print slides for sharing or as handouts.

Exercise

Exercise 1 – Choose the correct answer

1. Which tab do you use to insert a new slide in PowerPoint?
a) View
b) Home
c) Design
d) File
2. What is the purpose of the Slide Sorter view in PowerPoint?
a) To add animations to slides
b) To rearrange slides easily
c) To change the slide layout
d) To insert pictures

Exercise 2 – True/False

1. The Ribbon in PowerPoint contains all the tools and commands needed to create a presentation.
2. SmartArt diagrams cannot be edited after they are inserted into a slide.

Exercise 3- Assertion & Reason

1. Assertion: PowerPoint's AutoSave feature helps prevent data loss.
Reason: The AutoSave feature automatically saves the presentation every few minutes.
2. Assertion: Slide Show view allows you to edit individual slides.
Reason: Slide Show view is a mode where slides are shown in full screen.

Exercise 4- Jumble words

1. B O R N I B
2. E D I L S

Exercise 5- Short Questions

1. What is the purpose of using SmartArt in PowerPoint?
2. How can you add an audio clip to a slide in PowerPoint?

Answer

Exercise 1- 1. b) Home, 2. b) To rearrange slides easily
Exercise 2- 1. True, 2. False
Exercise 3- 1. Both assertion and reason are correct, and the reason explains the assertion.
2. The assertion is incorrect, but the reason is correct.
Exercise 4- 1. RIBBON,2. SLIDE

Project

Create a PowerPoint presentation that tells the story of a fun day in your life!

Activity

Solve the riddle: "I help you start fresh with a new page to share, Add me to keep your story fair and square.
What am I?"

Case Study

Your school is planning a special event, and you've been asked to create a presentation to introduce the different activities planned for the day. You'll need to create slides for each activity, add relevant images, and even insert audio clips for announcements.

Case Study Questions:

"What type of layout would best introduce each activity?"

"How can you ensure the presentation is organised so viewers can easily follow along?"
"What tools can you use to make the presentation engaging yet clear and easy to understand?"
"How would you handle technical issues, like sound not playing or slides not appearing correctly?"

Group Discussion

Discuss how PowerPoint can make learning more fun.

Chapter-3
TEST PAPER
Create Magic with PowerPoint

Time Duration: 20 Minutes **Maximum Marks: 10**

General Instructions:

1. The question paper consists of 10 questions.
2. All questions are compulsory.

True/False **(1 X 2 = 2 marks)**

1. You can add pictures to your PowerPoint slides using the Insert tab.
2. The Slide Sorter view is used to add animations to slides.

Choose the Correct Option **(1 X 3 = 3 marks)**

1. Which tab would you use to change the layout of a slide?
a) Insert
b) Design
c) Home
d) View
2. What is the purpose of the Ribbon in PowerPoint?
a) To save the presentation
b) To organise tools and options
c) To add new slides
d) To view all slides at once
3. Which feature allows you to add clickable shapes that perform an action when selected?
a) SmartArt
b) Action Button
c) Slide Sorter
d) Layout

Short Questions **(1 X 5 = 5 marks)**

1. What is the purpose of using SmartArt in a PowerPoint presentation?
2. How can you save your presentation to prevent losing your work?
3. Describe the steps to insert an audio clip in a PowerPoint slide.
4. Why might someone use the Slide Sorter view?
5. Explain how to add a new slide to an existing PowerPoint presentation.

Online Interactive Resources

	Online Exam Paper	**Chapter 3 Videos**
Link	https://forms.gle/9ZRaiMNJ5xcV67Qq7	https://www.youtube.com/playlist?list=PLzlh_31VWEFpbjoxFfHJ1mIHR5cbg__us

QR Code		

Half-Yearly Test Paper

Time Duration: 40 Minutes **Maximum Marks: 30**

General Instructions:

1. The question paper consists of 25 questions and is divided into four sections, A and B.
2. All questions are compulsory.
3. Section A comprises True/False, Fill in the blanks and one word of one mark each.
4. Section B comprises question numbers 1 to 5. These are Short Questions carrying two marks each.

SECTION-A

Fill in the Blanks **(1 X 10 = 10 marks)**

1. In a computer, data is stored in ________ and ________.
2. The basic unit to measure computer memory is ________.
3. ________ allows users to create, edit, and organise files and folders in Windows.
4. The ________ feature in Windows 11 helps you view all open windows and switch between them.
5. In PowerPoint, the ________ view shows all slides in a presentation as thumbnails.
6. ________ is used to add organised graphics like hierarchies and processes to a slide.
7. A ________ in PowerPoint allows you to link actions or navigate through slides.
8. To add a new folder, you can right-click and select ________ from the menu.
9. The shortcut for opening Task View in Windows 11 is ________ + ________.
10. When you save a PowerPoint presentation, it is saved with the extension ________.

True/False **(1 X 5 = 5 marks)**

1. SmartArt is a feature in PowerPoint that lets you add simple text only.
2. A folder is a place to store multiple files on a computer.
3. In Windows 11, right-clicking a file provides various options like rename, delete, and copy.
4. In PowerPoint, the "Exit" option closes the current presentation but keeps the software open.
5. RAM is a type of computer memory that stores data permanently.

One Word **(1 X 5 = 5 marks)**

1. What is the primary memory of a computer called?
2. Which tool in Windows allows you to see all open applications and windows?
3. In PowerPoint, what do you insert to organize visual information like charts and hierarchies?
4. What is the term for adding a new slide in PowerPoint?
5. Name the command that allows you to delete a file permanently.

SECTION-B

Short Questions **(2 X 5 = 10 marks)**

1. Explain the difference between computer memory and storage.
2. What is the purpose of creating folders in Windows, and how does it help in managing files?

3. Describe how to change the layout of a slide in PowerPoint.
4.Why is it important to save a presentation, and how can you open a saved presentation?
5. What are Action Buttons in PowerPoint, and how are they useful in a presentation?

Online Interactive Resources

Online Exam Paper:
Link: https://forms.gle/1jexicqcWJBjCWTv9

QR Code:

Chapter 4: Discover the Internet and Data Fun

In this chapter you will learn about:

- Internet services
- Information Retrieval
- Google Apps

The internet has become a part of our daily lives, making everything from communication to entertainment and education easily accessible. This chapter explores various internet services, teaches how to find information efficiently, introduces Google apps that simplify our tasks, and provides a glossary to help students understand key terms. The internet is not just a tool for fun but also a powerful resource for learning. This chapter will teach students how to make the most of the internet responsibly while enjoying the amazing world it offers.

4.1 Internet services

The Internet provides a wide range of services to meet the needs of people across the globe. Some services allow us to connect with others, while others offer education, shopping, entertainment, and much more. Let's explore some essential internet services:

Email (Electronic Mail):
Email is one of the earliest and most popular ways to send messages online.
With email, people can exchange text, images, videos, and documents.
Popular email providers include Gmail, Yahoo Mail, and Outlook.
Example: A teacher can send homework assignments to students via email.

Social Media Platforms:
Social media helps people share ideas, photos, and videos with friends and family in real time.
Platforms like Facebook, Instagram, and WhatsApp keep users connected.
Social media also serves as a source of news, trends, and entertainment.
Example: Sharing pictures of a vacation on Instagram allows friends to see and comment on them instantly.

Web Browsing:
A web browser is software like Google Chrome, Safari, or Mozilla Firefox that lets users explore websites.
You can access content on any topic using web browsers to explore the internet.
Example: A student searches for information on the solar system for a science project.

E-commerce (Online Shopping):
The internet has transformed how we shop. Websites like Amazon and Flipkart allow people to buy products from home.
E-commerce websites also offer services like home delivery, product reviews, and discounts.
Example: Parents order school supplies online and deliver them to their doorstep.

Streaming Services:

The internet allows us to watch videos, listen to music, and play games through streaming platforms.
YouTube, Netflix, and Spotify are popular streaming services.
Example: Students watch educational videos on YouTube to understand difficult concepts better.

Online Learning Platforms:
Education has become more accessible through online platforms such as Khan Academy, Byju's, and Google Classroom.
Students can attend virtual classes, complete assignments, and interact with teachers from anywhere.
Example: A student attends a math class online using Google Classroom.

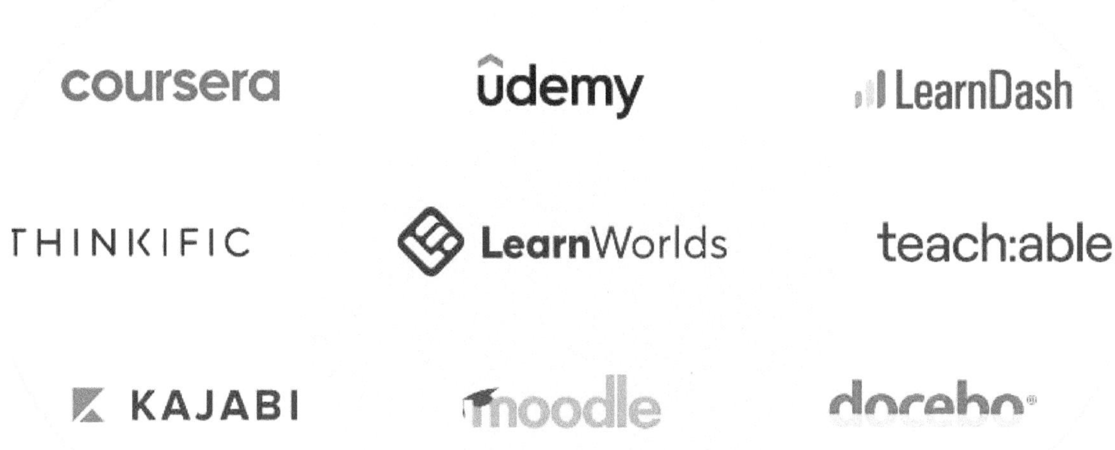

Cloud Storage Services:
Cloud storage enables people to store their data online and access it from any device.
Google Drive, OneDrive, and Dropbox are examples of cloud storage services.
Example: A student saves homework on Google Drive and accesses it from school.

Fun Fact:
The first website ever created is still live! It is a simple page created by Tim Berners-Lee, the inventor of the World Wide Web, in 1991.

4.2 Information Retrieval

Finding accurate information on the internet is important for students and professionals alike. However, knowing how to search efficiently helps save time and ensures we get the right information. Here's how we can improve our search skills:

Search Engines:
Search engines like Google, Bing, and Yahoo allow users to search for information by typing in words or phrases.
These tools quickly scan millions of websites to provide the most relevant results.

Using Keywords:
Keywords are the main words related to what you are searching for.
A good keyword helps search engines understand your query better.
Example: If you are searching for the history of bicycles, using "history of bicycles" will give better results than just "bicycles."

Tips for Better Searches:
Use quotation marks (" ") to search for an exact phrase.
Example: Searching "What is the speed of light" will give focused results.
Use a minus sign (-) before a word to exclude it from the search.
Example: "Jupiter -planet" will exclude information about the planet and give other relevant results.
Use specific terms: Adding more specific words narrows down the search.
Example: Searching for "solar system planets for kids" will give child-friendly content.

Identifying Reliable Information:
Look for websites with .edu, .gov, or .org domains since they usually offer trusted information.
Cross-check information from multiple sources to ensure accuracy.
Educational Websites:
Websites like National Geographic, Britannica, and NASA offer high-quality content.
These websites are useful for school projects and general knowledge.

Fun Fact:
Google answers more than 63,000 searches every second, making it the most used search engine worldwide!

4.3 Google Apps

Google offers a variety of apps that help students, teachers, and professionals organize tasks, store files, and communicate efficiently. Here are some popular Google apps and their uses:
Gmail:

Gmail is one of the most widely used email services.
It allows users to send and receive emails, organise inboxes, and schedule messages.
Google Drive:
Google Drive is a cloud storage service for storing photos, documents, and videos.
Files saved on Drive can be shared with others and accessed from anywhere.
Google Docs:
Google Docs allows users to create Word documents online.
Students and teachers can collaborate on the same document in real time.
Google Slides:
This app helps users create presentations with text, images, and videos.
It is a useful tool for students to present their school projects.
Google Maps:
Google Maps provides directions to places and helps people explore new locations.
It also shows traffic updates and estimated travel times.
Google Classroom:
Google Classroom is an online learning platform where teachers can assign homework and share materials with students.
YouTube:
YouTube offers various videos, from educational content to entertainment.
Google Calendar:
Google Calendar helps users organise their schedules and set reminders.
Fun Fact:
Google's original name was Backrub, but it was renamed Google in 1998 based on the mathematical term "googol," which means one followed by 100 zeros!

4.4 Glossary

Email: A way of sending messages electronically over the internet.
Web Browser: A program to access websites, such as Google Chrome.
Search Engine: A tool like Google that is used to find information online.
Social Media: Platforms that allow people to share and connect, like Instagram.
E-commerce: Buying and selling products or services online.
Cloud Storage: Saving files on the internet so that they can be accessed from any device.
Streaming: Watching videos or listening to music online without downloading them.
Google Drive: Google's cloud storage platform.
Reliable Information: Content that is accurate and trustworthy.
Google Maps: An app used to find directions and explore places.

4.5 Summary

The internet provides many services like email, social media, e-commerce, and streaming.
Information retrieval is essential, and search engines like Google help users find information quickly.
Using keywords and search tips can improve search accuracy and save time.

Google Apps offer communication, storage, and collaboration solutions with tools like Gmail, Google Drive, and Google Classroom.
Reliable information is critical; students must learn to identify trustworthy sources online.
Educational websites provide valuable resources for schoolwork and projects.
The internet offers endless possibilities, from connecting with friends to exploring new knowledge.

Exercise

Exercise 1 – Choose the correct answer

1. Which of the following is NOT a social media platform?
a) Instagram
b) Facebook
c) YouTube
d) Wikipedia
2. Which Google app is used for creating presentations?
a) Google Docs
b) Google Slides
c) Google Drive
d) Google Maps

Exercise 2 – True/False

1.YouTube is a streaming service that allows you to watch videos online.
2. Google Classroom is used to create documents and store them online.

Exercise 3- Rearrange the sentence

1. email / used / is / messages / to / send
2. explore / can / with / Maps / we / Google / places

Exercise 4- Choose the Odd One Out

1. Choose the odd one out:
a) Google Drive
b) Dropbox
c) Facebook
d) OneDrive
2. Choose the odd one out:
a) Google Docs
b) Google Slides
c) Google Classroom
d) Google Maps

Exercise 5- Short Questions

1. What is the purpose of Google Drive?

2. Name two ways we can retrieve information on the internet.

Answer

Exercise 1- 1. d) Wikipedia, 2. b) Google Slides
Exercise 2- 1. True, 2. False
Exercise 3- 1. Email is used to send messages. 2. We can explore places with Google Maps.
Exercise 4- 1. c) Facebook, 2.d) Google Maps

Project

Explore how the internet and Google Apps can be part of their daily lives.

Activity

Solve the riddles: I'm where your files stay—safe and sound, night and day. You can store docs, pics, and more. You can access me from any shore. **What am I?**

Case Study

Lily is a fourth-grade student who loves learning about space. One day, she has to do a project on planets, but she's not sure where to start. She opens her computer and searches online but finds too many sources. She also realises some information seems confusing. She tries Google Classroom, Google Docs, and Google Drive to organise her project.

Questions for Students:

How can Lily make sure she is using trustworthy sources for her project on planets?
What Google Apps could help Lily organise her project and save her work?
If Lily wants to share her project with her friends, which app should she use, and how?
What search tips could help Lily find accurate information quickly?

Group Discussion

Discuss how the internet and online tools impact their lives today and imagine their future uses.

Chapter-4
TEST PAPER
Discover the Internet and Data Fun

Time Duration: 20 Minutes **Maximum Marks: 10**

General Instructions:
1. The question paper consists of 10 questions.
2. All questions are compulsory.

True/False- **(1 X 2 = 2 marks)**
1. Google Maps is used for creating word documents.
2. Social media platforms allow people to connect and share content online.

Choose the Correct Option – **(1 X 3 = 3 marks)**
1. Which of the following is a cloud storage service?
a) Google Docs
b) Google Drive
c) YouTube
d) Gmail
2. Which Google app is used for writing and sharing documents online?
a) Google Classroom
b) Google Docs
c) Google Calendar
d) Google Maps
3. Which of these is NOT a search engine?
a) Google
b) Bing
c) Safari
d) Yahoo

Short Questions – **(1 X 5 = 5 marks)**
1. What is the purpose of Google Classroom?
2. Name two popular internet services used for communication.
3. How can you use Google Drive to store and share your files?
4. Why is it important to use reliable sources for information on the internet?
5. List any two Google Apps and describe their uses.

Online Interactive Resources

Online Exam Paper:
Link: https://forms.gle/Q6TW7hL9ZTDHQYpu9

QR Code:

Chapter 4 Videos Playlist:

Link: https://www.youtube.com/playlist?list=PLzlh_31VWEFod5u-jeTFkSpkpPoLmmkxg

QR Code:

Chapter 5: Become a Game Creator with Coding!

In this chapter you will learn about:

Start Coding with Scratch
Handle Events and Actions

Have you ever wondered how your favourite games are made? Creating games requires coding – giving computer instructions to make them do what you want! Learning to code is not just about games; it also helps develop problem-solving skills, logic, and creativity. For young learners, a platform like Scratch makes coding fun and easy.
This chapter will explore how to start coding with Scratch, understand events and actions, and dive into the joy of creating interactive games. Scratch allows you to drag and drop blocks instead of writing complicated code. In the glossary section, you will also learn some essential words used in game development. Let's get started and unleash your creativity!

5.1 Start Coding with Scratch

What is Scratch?
Scratch is a visual programming language designed for beginners, especially kids. With Scratch, you can create stories, games, and animations by arranging blocks of code. Instead of writing text-based code, you drag and snap blocks together like a puzzle.

Features of Scratch:
Blocks-based coding: No need to memorize complex code.
Sprites: Characters or objects in your game or animation.
Stage: The area where the game or animation takes place.
Costumes: Different appearances for your sprites.
Sounds: Add music or sound effects to your game.
Backdrops: Change the background of your stage to match the theme of your game.
Online Community: Share your projects and see other learners' creations.

Steps to Start Coding with Scratch:
Open Scratch: You can use the Scratch software or visit scratch.mit.edu online.
Create a New Project: Click on 'Create' to start a new project.
Select a Sprite: Choose a character (sprite) or draw your own.
Choose a Backdrop: Pick a background for your game or scene.
Drag and Drop Blocks: Use code blocks to make your sprite move, talk, or interact.
Test Your Game: Play your game to see how it works, then make changes to improve it.

Fun Fact:
The MIT Media Lab developed scratch to help children learn to code creatively. It is now used by millions of students worldwide.

5.2 Handle Events and Actions

What Are Events and Actions?

In coding, **events** are triggers that start actions. For example, pressing a key or clicking the mouse triggers something to happen in your game. Actions are the things that happen in response to these events, such as a sprite moving or changing colours.

Common Events in Scratch:

When Green Flag Clicked: Starts the game or animation.
When Key Pressed: Something happens when a specific key is pressed (e.g., move up with the arrow key).
When Sprite Clicked: A character acts when clicked.
Broadcast Message: Send messages to other sprites to trigger actions.

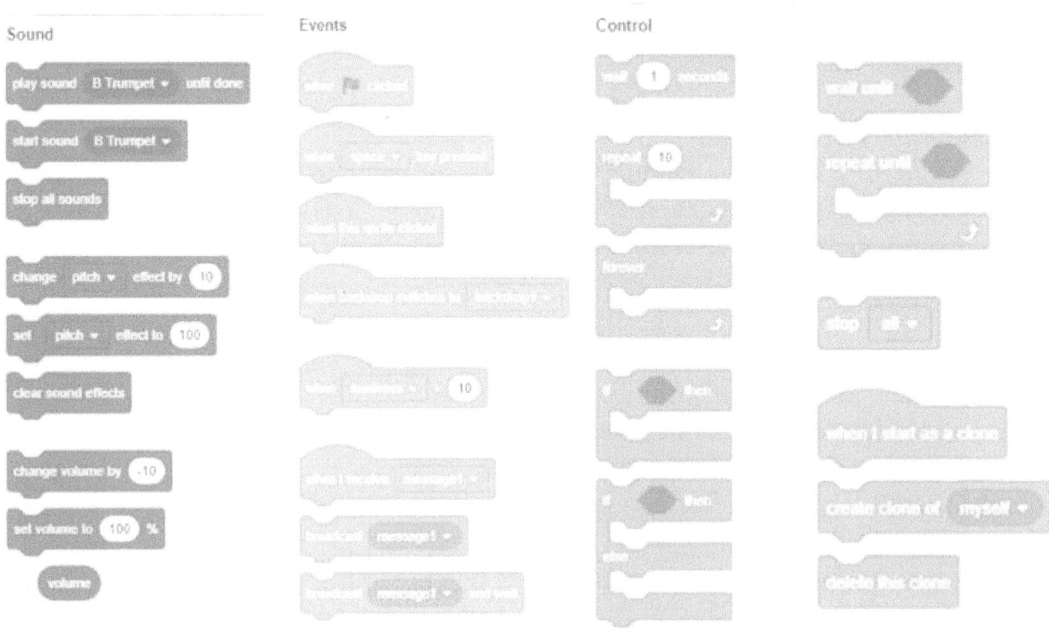

Everyday Actions in Scratch:

Move: Make your sprite move left, right, up, or down.
Speak: Display text bubbles or make your sprite talk.
Change Costumes: Switch between different appearances.
Play Sound: Add sound effects or background music.
Repeat (Loops): Make an action happen multiple times.

Activity: Create a Simple Game

Let's create a basic game where the player controls a sprite using the arrow keys.
Choose a Sprite (e.g., a cat).
Add Key Press Events (e.g., move right when the right arrow is pressed).
Set Actions (e.g., play a sound when the sprite reaches the edge).
Test and Improve Your Game.

Fun Fact:
Many programmers started their careers by building simple games using Scratch!

5.3 Glossary

Coding: Writing instructions for computers to follow.
Block-based Coding: Programming using visual blocks instead of text.
Sprite: Characters or objects in a Scratch project.
Stage: The area where the game or animation takes place.
Backdrop: The background of the stage.
Costume: Different looks for a sprite.
Event: An action that triggers something to happen (e.g., key press).
Action: What happens when an event occurs (e.g., sprite moves).
Loop: A block that repeats an action multiple times.
Broadcast: Sending messages between sprites to trigger events.

5.4 Summary

Scratch is a visual programming tool that makes coding fun and easy.
With block-based coding, students can create games, animations, and stories.
Sprites are the characters or objects in a Scratch project, while the stage is where everything happens.
Events trigger actions in the game. For example, pressing a key or clicking a sprite can start an action.
Actions are the responses to events, such as a sprite moving or playing a sound.
Loops allow actions to repeat multiple times, making games more interactive.
Broadcasting messages between sprites helps in creating advanced interactions.
Coding with Scratch encourages creativity, problem-solving, and logical thinking.
By exploring Scratch, students can build their games and share them with the Scratch online community.
Learning to code through games prepares students for more advanced programming languages in the future.

Exercise

Exercise 1 – Choose the Correct Answer
1. What is Scratch mainly used for?
a) Drawing pictures
b) Creating stories, games, and animations
c) Listening to music
d) Sending emails
2. In Scratch, which of these is NOT an event?

a) When Green Flag Clicked
b) When Sprite Clicked
c) When Costume Changed
d) When Key Pressed

Exercise 2 – True/False
1. Scratch uses text-based coding for creating projects.
2. In Scratch, a "sprite" refers to the background of a project.

Exercise 3 – Rearrange the Sentence
1. blocks, Scratch, code, uses, to, with, create
2. move, allows, arrow, sprites, The, keys, to, in, game, a

Exercise 4 – Assertion & Reason
1. **Assertion:** Scratch is a programming language designed for beginners.
Reason: Scratch uses visual blocks instead of text-based coding, making it easier for kids to learn.
a. Both Assertion and Reason are true, and Reason is the correct explanation of Assertion.
b. Both Assertion and Reason are true, but Reason is not the correct explanation of Assertion.
c. Assertion is true, but Reason is false.
d. Assertion is false, and Reason is true.

2. **Assertion:** Sprites in Scratch can only move in one direction.
Reason: Scratch limits sprite movements to up and down only.
a. Both Assertion and Reason are true, and Reason is the correct explanation of Assertion.
b. Both Assertion and Reason are true, but Reason is not the correct explanation of Assertion.
c. Assertion is true, but Reason is false.
d. Assertion is false, and Reason is true.

Exercise 5 – Short Questions
1. What is a "sprite" in Scratch, and how is it used in a project?
2. Explain the role of "events" in a Scratch project. Give an example.

Answer

Exercise 1- 1. b) Creating stories, games, and animations. 2. c) When Costume Changed
Exercise 2- 1. False, 2. False
Exercise 3- 1. Scratch uses blocks to create code. 2. The arrow keys allow sprites to move in a game.
Exercise 4- 1. a) Both Assertion and Reason are true, and Reason is the correct explanation of Assertion.
2. d) Assertion is false, and Reason is true.

Project

Build a simple interactive game using Scratch where players control a character to collect points.

Activity

Design a game where a character (sprite) has to avoid obstacles and reach the goal.

Case Study

Meet Arjun and Aanya, two young friends who love playing games. One day, they decided they wanted to make their own game. They found Scratch, a platform that lets them create their own games, stories, and animations. As they start creating, they face challenges: Arjun struggles with coding blocks, while Aanya finds it difficult to choose the right sprites. Together, they work hard, learn to use Scratch, and finally create a game they can play and share with friends.

Case Study Questions:
What challenges did Arjun and Aanya face while creating their game?
How did Arjun and Aanya help each other to solve their problems?
Have you ever faced a challenge while creating something? How did you overcome it?

Group Discussion

Discuss why learning coding is fun and beneficial and how it helps in various aspects of life.

Chapter-5
TEST PAPER
Become a Game Creator with Coding!

Time Duration: 20 Minutes **Maximum Marks: 10**

General Instructions:

1. The question paper consists of 10 questions.
2. All questions are compulsory.

True/False- **(1 X 2 = 2 marks)**

1. Scratch is a text-based programming language designed for professional programmers.
2. In Scratch, a "sprite" is an object or character that can perform actions in a project.

Choose the Correct Option **(1 X 3 = 3 marks)**

1. Which of the following is a feature of Scratch?
a) Writing code by typing text
b) Drag-and-drop blocks
c) Only works offline
d) Requires complex math
2. In Scratch, what creates different appearances for a sprite?
a) Backgrounds
b) Sounds
c) Costumes
d) Loops
3. Which block would you use to make a sprite move when clicking the green flag?
a) When Space Key Pressed
b) Repeat Until
c) When Green Flag Clicked
d) Change Costume

Short Questions **(1 X 5 = 5 marks)**

1. What is Scratch, and why is it suitable for beginners?
2. Explain what an "event" is in Scratch, with an example.
3. How can sprites interact with each other in a Scratch project?
4. Describe the role of the "stage" in a Scratch project.
5. What is the purpose of the "repeat" or "loop" block in Scratch coding?

Online Interactive Resources

Online Exam Paper:
Link: https://forms.gle/ugTmp7JB4tiVaQ5T6

QR Code:

Chapter 6 Videos Playlist:

Link: https://www.youtube.com/playlist?list=PLzlh_31VWEFq0_45xkXnf05XxeQkpppb_

QR Code:

Chapter 6: Viva Voce

9.1 Question and Answer

Q 1: What does the bold text do?
A: It makes the text thicker and darker.

Q 2: What is cloud storage?
A: Cloud storage allows you to save your files online, accessible from any device with the internet.

Q 3: What is a printer used for?
A: A printer prints documents or pictures from a computer onto paper.

Q 4: How do you insert a shape in MS Word?
A: Go to the "Insert" tab and choose "Shapes."

Q 5: Why should you press the keys gently on a keyboard?
A: To keep the computer in good shape and avoid damaging the keys.

Q 6: What is a font in MS Word?
A: A font is the style in which the text appears.

Q 7: How do games help you learn?
A: Some games teach math, science, and problem-solving while you play.

Q 8: What is a storage device?
A: A device where digital information is saved for future use.

Q 9: What is the CPU?
A: The CPU is the computer's brain, helping it think and solve problems.

Q 10: Why should you sit appropriately while using a computer?
A: Sitting properly helps prevent strain on your neck and keeps you comfortable.

Q 11: What do speakers do?
A: Speakers produce sound from the computer, like music or video audio.

Q 12: Why should you not eat or drink near a computer?
A: Food crumbs and liquids can damage the computer.

Q 13: What is the difference between hardware and software?
A: Hardware is the physical part of a computer, and software is the programs that make it work.

Q 14: What is the Internet?
A: The Internet is a global network of computers that share information.

Q 15: What does a word processor do?
A: It helps you write and edit text on the computer.

Q 16: What is personal information?
A: Personal information includes your name, address, school, or phone number.

Q 17: Why should you keep your password safe?
A: To protect your private accounts and information.

Q 18: How do you change the text colour in MS Word?
A: Highlight the text, click the text colour button, and choose a colour from the dropdown menu.

Q 19: What does the monitor do?
A: It displays everything on the computer, like text and videos.

Q 20: What is external storage?
A: Storage devices connected to a computer, like USB or external hard drives.

Online Interactive Resources

Online Exam Paper:
Link: https://forms.gle/Rh2dXDzHrS8SFdKt5

QR Code:

Chapter 6 Videos Playlist:
Link: https://www.youtube.com/playlist?list=PLzlh_31VWEFrJ_l8zVyfDXR2i8iseEto8

QR Code:

Chapter 7: More about Artificial Intelligence

Artificial Intelligence, or AI, is a special technology that helps machines like computers and robots think and learn like humans. It is becoming a big part of our lives. You may not realise it, but AI is all around us! From the voice assistants on our phones to the recommendations we get when watching videos online, AI is working silently to make things easier and more fun for us.

One way AI works is by helping machines to recognise things. Have you ever noticed how your phone camera can detect faces when you take a picture? That is AI at work! AI can also recognise animals, objects, or even your voice. When you say, "Hey Siri" or "OK Google," your phone understands and answers because of AI.

AI also helps computers and machines learn from the past. Consider how you learn things in school—practising and remembering what works best. AI does something similar. It can look at old information, learn from it, and make better decisions next time. For example, if you watch a lot of cartoons on YouTube, the app will suggest more cartoons for you to watch. It remembers what you like and gives you more of it.

AI can also play games with you! Some video games you enjoy use AI to create characters that play against you. These characters can be brilliant because they learn how to win from playing with you. If you try one move, the game might respond with an even better move to challenge you. Isn't that cool?

AI is also used in cars to make driving safer. Some new cars have AI systems that can drive the car without the help of a person. These are called self-driving cars. The AI in these cars watches the road, sees the traffic lights, and even stops if a person or animal suddenly crosses the road.

AI helps in schools, too! Some teachers use special AI tools to understand how well students are learning. These tools can tell teachers what each student needs help with so they can teach better. Imagine having a personal robot teacher who knows exactly where you need extra practice—that's what AI can do!

Even doctors use AI. It helps them look at pictures like X-rays to determine if someone is sick. AI can find signs of illness much faster than a person can. This allows doctors to give better treatment to people.

Another fantastic thing about AI is how it can understand different languages. Some phone apps can translate words from one language to another in just a few seconds. So, if you meet someone who speaks a different language, AI can help you understand each other better.

AI is used to keep us safe online, too. It helps in blocking harmful messages or destructive content on the internet. Apps like WhatsApp and Facebook use AI to detect and stop spam messages or fake news from spreading. This makes the internet a safer place to explore and learn.

AI makes life more exciting and comfortable, but it also comes with responsibilities. We need to use it wisely. For example, we should never depend only on AI for everything. Sometimes, it is essential to think for ourselves and make our own decisions.

In the future, AI will become even smarter. Some people believe that robots with AI might help with house chores or even become friends who can talk with us. AI could help solve big problems, like finding cures for diseases or assisting farmers to grow more food. It is like having an intelligent assistant to work with people to improve the world.

Even though AI is mighty, it is essential to remember that humans make it. It learns from the things we teach it. That means we need to be careful and prepare it good things. If we use AI correctly, it can do beautiful things for us. But if we use it carelessly, it might create problems. So, learning about AI and using it correctly is vital for everyone.

AI is a magical world of possibilities. From your favourite games to the cars of the future, AI will keep growing and becoming a more significant part of our lives. Isn't it exciting to imagine what AI might do next? Maybe one day, you will even create your own AI robot or app to help people! The future is full of endless opportunities with AI, and it all begins with learning and understanding how it works today.

Online Interactive Resources

Online Exam Paper:
Link: https://forms.gle/6zgyoHSSveVqhqj78

QR Code:

Chapter 7 Videos Playlist:
Link: https://www.youtube.com/playlist?list=PLzlh_31VWEFq7xu2dV6TJmoVae8LJaV1R

QR Code:

Chapter 8: AI in Daily Life

In this chapter, you will learn about:
Real-life Examples of AI
Virtual Assistant
AI in Entertainment
AI in Everyday Life

8.1 Understanding Real-Life Examples of Artificial Intelligence (AI)

AI is present in many of the technologies we rely on daily, making tasks more efficient and personalised. For instance, virtual assistants like Siri, Alexa, and Google Assistant can understand and respond to voice commands, assisting with setting reminders, playing music, and managing smart devices. Self-driving cars utilise AI to navigate safely, avoid obstacles, and make driving decisions independently, enhancing both safety and efficiency in transportation. In smart homes, AI powers devices like thermostats and lights, learning user preferences to create a comfortable environment. Additionally, AI in entertainment suggests movies, music, and games based on your interests, helping you discover content tailored to your taste. These examples highlight how AI enhances convenience, safety, and personalisation in our everyday lives.

Now, let's explore each example in more detail.

8.2 Virtual Assistant

A virtual assistant is an intelligent computer program that helps you with tasks by understanding what you say or type. It uses Artificial Intelligence (AI) to listen to your commands, figure out what you want, and do it for you. You can find virtual assistants at home on your phone, computer, or even smart speakers. They make everyday tasks easier, like setting reminders, playing music, or controlling lights in your house.

Siri

Siri is Apple's virtual assistant, available on iPhones, iPads, Macs, and other Apple devices. To activate Siri, simply say, "Hey, Siri," followed by your command. For example, to check the weather, you could ask, "What's the weather today?" Siri will then retrieve and share the current weather conditions. Over time, Siri learns from your habits, such as frequently used apps or contacts, to provide more personalized suggestions and assistance.

Examples of tasks Siri can handle:

Setting reminders and alarms.
Sending messages or making calls.
Giving directions or finding locations.
Controlling smart home devices like lights or thermostats.
Playing music or podcasts.

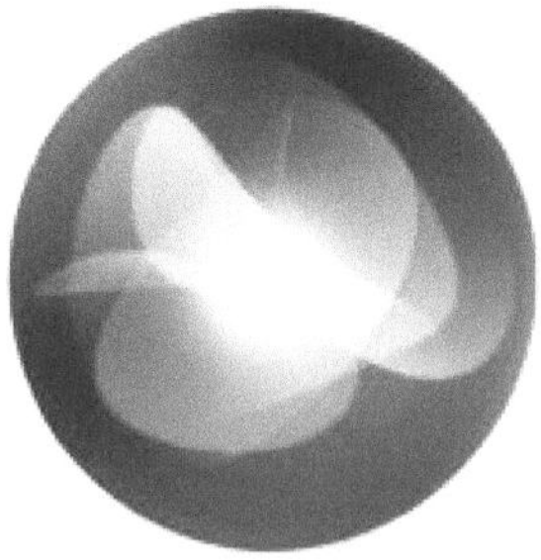

Alexa
Alexa is Amazon's virtual assistant on devices like the Amazon Echo and other smart speakers. To use Alexa, you start by saying, "Alexa," followed by your request. For example, you can say, "Alexa, play my favourite playlist," and Alexa will play the music that matches your taste. Alexa can also control various smart devices in your home, like turning on lights, adjusting the thermostat, or locking doors. Over time, Alexa learns from your commands and becomes better at helping you with tasks.

Examples of tasks Alexa can do:
Play music or read audiobooks.
Control smart home devices.
Answer questions by searching the internet.
Provide news updates and weather forecasts.
Set timers and alarms.

Virtual assistants like Siri and Alexa are examples of how AI is used to make our lives more convenient and personalised.

8.3 AI in entertainment
AI is used in entertainment to make games, movies, and music more fun and exciting. It helps create realistic characters in video games, recommends films and songs you might like, and even helps artists create new music. AI can learn what you enjoy and suggest more things that match your tastes.

Movie recommendations
AI tracks what you've watched and enjoyed when you watch movies or TV shows on platforms like Netflix, Disney+, or Amazon Prime. It uses this information to recommend other movies or shows you like. For example, AI will suggest similar films if you enjoy

superhero movies. This makes finding something fun to watch easier without spending a lot of time searching.

How AI helps:
Analyze your viewing history.
Suggests movies or shows that match your interests.
Keep your recommendations updated as your tastes change.

Video game characters

In video games, AI controls the behaviour of non-player characters (NPCs). These characters can interact with you in the game, making the experience more realistic and challenging. For example, AI might control other drivers in a racing game, making the race more exciting by adapting their driving styles to challenge you.

Examples of AI in games:
AI opponents in racing or shooting games.
Characters that react to your decisions in role-playing games.
Adaptive difficulty levels that match your skill level.

Music Suggestions

Music streaming apps like Spotify use AI to recommend songs and playlists based on your listening habits. When you listen to a song, the AI learns what music you enjoy and suggests similar songs. This way, you can discover new music that matches your taste without searching for it.

How AI helps:
Curates personalised playlists based on your listening history.
Recommends new artists and songs that you might like.
Updates suggestions as your music.

Social media

AI is also used in social media platforms like Instagram, Facebook, Twitter, etc. It helps show posts, ads, and content that match your interests. AI looks at what you view, like, comment on, and share and then suggests more of the same type of content.

Examples of AI in social media:
Recommends posts and videos that match your interests.
Filters out unwanted or inappropriate content.

Suggests friends or accounts you might want to follow.

AI in entertainment helps create personalised experiences, making finding content you'll love easier.

8.4 AI in everyday life

AI is not just limited to entertainment and virtual assistants; it also plays a vital role in everyday life, from typing messages to managing your smartphone's battery. Here are some examples:

Voice typing

Voice typing is a feature on smartphones and computers that uses AI to convert your speech into text. Instead of typing out a message or document, you can speak, and the AI will transcribe your words into text on the screen. This feature is handy for people with difficulty typing or needing to write something quickly.

Examples of Voice typing:

Dictating messages or emails.
Writing notes or documents by speaking.
Voice commands to search the web or control apps.

Battery management

Some smartphones use AI to manage battery life more efficiently. The AI learns how you use your phone throughout the day and adjusts power settings to make the battery last longer. For example, if you use your phone heavily in the evening, the AI might conserve power during the day to ensure you have enough battery life later.

How AI helps:

Analyses your phone usage patterns.

Adjusts brightness, background processes, and other settings.
Extends battery life by optimising power consumption.

Smart home devices
AI is used in various smart home devices, like thermostats, lights, security systems, etc. These devices learn your habits and preferences and automatically adjust settings to make your home more comfortable and secure. For example, a smart thermostat might know that you like it warmer in the morning and cooler at night and will adjust the temperature accordingly.

Examples of AI in smart homes:
Smart thermostats that learn your temperature preferences.
Automated lighting systems that adjust based on the time of day.
Security systems that recognise familiar faces and alert you to strangers.

Smartphones
AI enhances smartphone cameras by automatically adjusting settings like focus, lighting, and filters to improve your photos. For example, when photographing a sunset, the AI might enhance the colours to make the sky look more vibrant and beautiful.

How AI helps:
Improves photo quality by adjusting camera settings.
Recognises faces and objects to focus better.
Suggests filters and effects to enhance your photos.

Online shopping
When you shop online, AI helps you find products you might like by analysing your browsing and purchase history. It suggests items similar to what you've bought or searched for, making your shopping experience more personalised.

Examples of AI in online shopping:
Recommends products based on your past purchases.
Suggests items that other customers with similar tastes have bought.
Personalizes your shopping experience with targeted ads and offers.

AI is everywhere, from the devices we use to the services we enjoy. It helps us make tasks easier, improve convenience, and provide personalised experiences. By understanding how AI works in daily life, you can better appreciate the technology that powers our world and even think about how you might use AI to solve problems in the future.

8.5 Glossary

Virtual assistant: An intelligent program (like Siri or Alexa) that helps with tasks using voice commands.
Entertainment AI: AI used in games and movies to make them more fun and personalised.
Social media AI: AI that shows you posts and ads based on what you like on platforms like Instagram.
Smart home devices: AI-powered gadgets that learn your preferences and automate things like lighting and temperature in your home.
Online shopping: Buying products online with AI suggesting items based on preferences.
Personalization: AI tailoring services to individual preferences.

8.6 Summary

AI allows machines to perform tasks requiring Human Intelligence, like learning and decision-making.
AI is present in virtual assistants, self-driving cars, and smart home devices, enhancing convenience and safety.
Siri and Alexa use AI to help with tasks through voice commands.
AI suggests movies and music and improves video game experiences based on user preferences.
AI helps with voice typing, battery management, smart home automation, and personalised online shopping.

Exercise

Exercise 1 – Choose the correct answer from the given options.

1. What is an example of AI in everyday life?
a) Virtual assistants like Siri and Alexa
b) Manual typewriters
c) Analog clocks
d) Traditional radios
2. How do self-driving cars use AI?
a) To play music
b) To navigate roads safely without human intervention
c) To charge their batteries
d) To display advertisements

Exercise 2 – Check if the sentence is true or false.

1. AI is only used in computers...................
2. Virtual assistants like Siri and Alexa can respond to voice commands...................

Exercise 3 – Fill the blank space with the correct word.

1. AI improves ...., safety and personalisation in our everyday lives.
2. Virtual assistants like Siri use .... to understand and respond to voice commands.

Exercise 4- Solve the jumbled word by arranging the letters.

1. RISI (Hint: Apple's virtual assistant)
2. XEALA (Hint: Amazon's virtual assistant)

Exercise 5- Answer the following questions in your own words.

1. How does AI make tasks more efficient in our everyday lives?
2. Give an example of how AI is used in smart home devices.

Answer

Exercise 1- 1. a) 2. b)
Exercise 2- 1. False 2. True
Exercise 3- 1. convenience 2. AI
Exercise 4- 1. Siri 2. Alexa

Project

Exploring AI in everyday life

This is to help students understand how AI (Artificial Intelligence) is integrated into various aspects of everyday life, such as virtual assistants, entertainment, and smart home devices.

Activity

Activity: AI scavenger hunt
Objective:
To engage students in understanding the practical applications of AI through fun and interactive activities.

Materials needed:
Smartphones or tablets (optional)
Printed scavenger hunt list
Pens or pencils

Instructions:
Introduction to the activity:
Explain to the students that they will be going on an "AI Scavenger Hunt" to find examples of AI in their surroundings, either at home or in the classroom.

Create the scavenger hunt list:
Prepare a list of AI-related items or activities for the students to find. Examples:
Find a device that uses a virtual assistant like Siri or Alexa.
Spot a smart home device that controls temperature, lights, or security.
Identify an app that recommends movies, music, or products on your phone.
Locate a feature in your smartphone that uses AI to enhance photos.
Identify a game that uses AI to control characters or opponents.
If this is done at home, students can check with their parents to find these items.

The hunt:
Give each student or group a scavenger hunt list.
Students will have a set amount of time (e.g., 20-30 minutes) to find as many items as possible on the list.
For each item found, students should write down what it is and how AI is used.

Sharing and discussion:
After the scavenger hunt, gather the students to share what they found.
Discuss how each AI example they found works and why it's useful.
Ask students to think about other places or devices where they might discover AI in action.

Case Study

AI super school

In a futuristic school, 12-year-old Arjun is amazed at how much AI is involved in his everyday learning. His classes feel like they are made just for him; the school's robots take care of all the tedious chores, and the AI can even predict when he's about to struggle with his homework. Arjun is curious: How do these systems work, and can they understand what he needs better than he does? He begins his adventure to discover the answers.

Group Discussion

How AI is used in everyday life

Students will discuss how AI is used in everyday life, such as smartphones, smart home devices, virtual assistants, and entertainment. They will explore how AI makes tasks like setting reminders, improving photos, and finding movies or music more accessible and personalised.

Discussion points:

What are some examples of AI that you use every day?

How does AI help make tasks more accessible at home or school?

Do you think AI is helpful, or are there any challenges or concerns?

How might AI continue to change the way we live in the future?

Chapter-8
TEST PAPER
AI in Daily Life

Time Duration: 20 Minutes **Maximum Marks: 10**

General Instructions:
1. The question paper consists of 10 questions.
2. All questions are compulsory.

I - Choose the correct answer from the given options. **(1 X 2 = 2 marks)**

1. What is a virtual assistant?
a) An intelligent computer program that helps you with different tasks
b) A physical robot that cleans your house
c) A video game character
d) A calculator

2. Which company developed Siri?
a) Amazon
b) Google
c) Apple
d) Microsoft

II - Fill the blank space with the correct word. **(1 X 3 = 3 marks)**

1. AI can help in __________ languages instantly, making it easier to communicate with people who speak _____________ languages.
2. In online shopping, AI helps by __________ products that you might like based on your previous searches and purchases.

III - Answer the following questions in your own words. **(3 X 4 = 12 marks)**

1. How does AI assist in creating realistic animations in movies?
2. What role does AI play in video games to enhance the gaming experience?
3. In what way does AI contribute to improving navigation and finding routes in real time?
4. What do you call the AI feature that helps translate languages instantly?
5. What is the term for AI suggesting products based on your shopping habits?

Online Interactive Resources

Online Exam Paper:
Link: https://forms.gle/zP6s7Tcm33awGcbi9

QR Code:

Chapter 8 Videos Playlist:

Link: https://www.youtube.com/playlist?list=PLzlh_31VWEFp5dd-lGgA7wm5WrjJ1XZpC

QR Code:

Chapter 9: Augmented & Virtual Reality

In this chapter you will learn about:
Introduction to AR and VR
Difference between AI and VR
Use of AR in Daily Lives
Computer Vision
Applications of Computer Vision

9.1 Introduction to AR and VR

Two exciting concepts in technology are changing how we experience the world: Augmented Reality (AR) and Virtual Reality (VR). These technologies allow us to see and interact with digital objects in new ways. In this chapter, we will explore what AR and VR are, how they work, and how they are used in our daily lives.

What is Augmented Reality (AR)?
Augmented Reality (AR) is a technology that overlays digital information—such as images, sounds, or other data—onto the real world. This means you can see and interact with digital objects while being aware of your surroundings.
Imagine using your smartphone camera to view your classroom. With AR, you might see virtual animals walking around your classroom or arrows pointing to different objects, providing information about them. The real world is still there, but it's enhanced with these digital additions.

Examples of Augmented Reality (AR):
AR Games: Games like PokÈmon GO use AR to place virtual characters in real-world environments. You can see PokÈmon on your phone screen when you play as if they were right before you.
AR in Education: AR apps can bring textbooks to life by showing 3D models, animations, and additional information when you point your device at a page.
AR in Shopping: Some apps let you use AR to see how furniture or decorations will look in your home before you buy them. You can point your phone at a spot in your room, and the app will show a virtual version of the item in place.

How does Augmented Reality (AR) work?
AR uses a device like a smartphone or tablet camera to capture the real world. Then, it uses software to add digital objects to the scene. This could be anything from a virtual character to a

piece of information. The device's screen combines the natural world and digital objects, creating an augmented experience.

What is Virtual Reality (VR)?

Virtual Reality (VR) is a technology that creates a completely immersive digital environment. When you put on a VR headset, you are taken into a virtual world that feels real, even though it's entirely computer-generated. Everything you see and hear in VR is part of this digital world; you can interact with it just like in the real world.

When you wear a VR headset, you might find yourself exploring an underwater world, flying through space, or playing inside a video game. In VR, the real world is replaced by this digital environment, and you feel like you're genuinely there.

Examples of VR:

VR games: In VR games, you can explore virtual worlds, interact with objects, and even feel like you are part of the action. For example, you might play a game where you explore space, fly a spaceship, or fight virtual enemies.

VR in education: VR can take virtual field trips to places like ancient Egypt or outer space. You can explore these environments as if you were there.

VR in training: Professionals like pilots, doctors, and firefighters use VR to practice their skills in a safe, controlled environment. For example, a pilot can practice flying in a virtual aeroplane before taking off in a real one.

How VR works:

VR uses a headset with screens in front of your eyes to create the illusion of being in a different place. The headset tracks your head movements, so when you look around, the virtual environment moves with you, making it feel like you are there. VR can also use hand controllers to let you interact with virtual objects, like picking up a ball or opening a virtual door.

AR and VR are becoming more popular in games, education, and even shopping, making these activities more fun and interactive. While AR adds to the real world, VR creates a new world to explore.

9.2 The History and Evolution of AR and VR

Understanding AR and VR technologies' origins and evolution over time is essential for fully appreciating them.

Early beginnings

Stereoscopic viewers (1838): Creating a three-dimensional (3D) experience began in the 19th century with the invention of stereoscopic viewers. These devices used two slightly different images viewed through lenses to create a 3D effect, which laid the groundwork for future virtual experiences.

The Sensorama (1962): Morton Heilig invented the Sensorama, one of the earliest attempts at creating a virtual reality experience. The Sensorama machine combined 3D video with smells, vibrations, and sounds to create an immersive experience. Although it wasn't interactive, it was a precursor to modern VR.

Development of AR and VR Technologies

Virtual Reality in the 1960s and 70s: The idea of VR started to take shape with the development of the first head-mounted displays (HMDs) in the 1960s. A computer scientist, Ivan Sutherland created the "Sword of Damocles," the first HMD that displayed basic computer graphics. However, it was heavy and required a lot of equipment to operate.

Early Augmented Reality (1990s): Tom Caudell coined the term "Augmented Reality" in the 1990s while working at Boeing. He used AR to help workers visualise how to assemble aircraft parts by overlaying digital instructions onto real-world components.

Gaming and consumer interest (1990s): The 1990s saw the first commercial attempts to bring VR to consumers, particularly in gaming. Companies like Sega and Nintendo released VR headsets, but they were limited by the technology of the time, offering low-quality graphics and a poor user experience.

Modern advancements

Smartphones and AR (2008-2010s): The introduction of smartphones with advanced cameras, sensors, and processing power enabled the development of AR apps. Apps like Snapchat and PokÈmon GO brought AR into the mainstream by allowing users to interact with virtual objects overlaid on the natural world through their phones.

Consumer VR (2010s-present): The 2010s saw a resurgence in VR with the development of more affordable and powerful VR headsets like the Oculus Rift, HTC Vive, and PlayStation VR. These devices provided high-quality VR experiences, making the technology more accessible to consumers.

Mixed Reality (MR): In addition to AR and VR, a new technology called Mixed Reality (MR) emerged. MR combines elements of both AR and VR, allowing natural and virtual objects to interact with each other in real-time. Microsoft's HoloLens is one example of an MR device that overlays holographic images onto the natural world and lets users interact with them.

9.3 Difference Between AI and VR

Artificial Intelligence (AI) and Virtual Reality (VR) are essential technologies with different roles and uses. Let's understand the difference between them:

Aspect	Artificial Intelligence (AI)	Virtual Reality (VR)
Definition	AI is like the brain of a machine, enabling computers to think, learn, and make decisions.	VR creates an entirely new and immersive digital environment.
Function	Allows computers to analyse data, recognise patterns, and solve problems like humans.	It places users into an authentic digital world, even though it's entirely computer-generated.
Purpose	It makes machines intelligent enough to perform tasks requiring human-like thought.	Creates an immersive experience where users can interact with a virtual environment.
Interaction	AI interacts with data and makes decisions based on that data.	VR allows users to interact with a virtual environment.
Application	Used in smart devices, data analysis, games, and more.	Used in gaming, education, training, and simulations.
Hardware	Runs on computers, smartphones, and other smart devices.	Requires VR headsets and controllers.

They serve different purposes but can be combined to create even more advanced technologies.

9.4 The Science Behind AR and VR

Let's examine the basic science and technology behind AR and VR to understand better how they work.

The Technology of Augmented Reality (AR)

Cameras and sensors: AR relies on cameras and sensors to capture the real-world environment. The camera on your smartphone or tablet acts as the AR system's eyes, capturing everything around you.

Processing power: Once the real-world environment is captured, the device's processor analyses the data to identify surfaces, objects, and the context in which digital elements should be placed. This analysis happens in real time, so the digital elements appear instantly on your screen.

Graphics and display: The device then overlays digital graphics onto the real-world image captured by the camera. These graphics can be anything from simple text to complex 3D models, and they move and change as you move the device, maintaining the illusion that they are part of the real world.

Tracking and mapping: AR systems use advanced algorithms to track your movements and the camera's position. This allows digital objects to stay in place relative to the real world, even as you move around.

The Technology of Virtual Reality (VR)

VR headsets: A VR headset is the most important piece of equipment for experiencing VR. It has two small screens inside, one for each eye, that create a 3D image by displaying slightly different views of the virtual environment to each eye, just like how our eyes see the real world.

Motion tracking: VR headsets have sensors that track head movements. When you turn your head, the view in the VR world changes just as it would in the real world. Some VR systems also include hand controllers that track hand movement, allowing you to interact with objects in the virtual environment.

Sound and haptics: To make VR experiences even more immersive, many VR systems include headphones that provide 3D audio, making sounds come from the right direction as they would in the real world. Some advanced VR systems also use haptic feedback, which means the controllers or other devices vibrate or provide resistance, so you can "feel" virtual objects.

Rendering and simulation: The VR system's processor and graphics card work together to create the virtual environment. This involves rendering 3D graphics, simulating physics (like gravity and collision), and ensuring the experience runs smoothly without lag.

9.5 Benefits and Challenges of AR and VR

While AR and VR offer many exciting possibilities, they also have some challenges. Let's explore both the benefits and the obstacles of these technologies.

Benefits of AR and VR

Enhanced learning: AR and VR make learning more engaging and effective by providing interactive and immersive experiences. Students can explore historical sites, conduct virtual experiments, or travel inside the human body.

Improved training: VR can be used for safe, risk-free training by professionals in medicine, aviation, and the military. For example, surgeons can practice complex operations in a virtual environment before performing them on actual patients.

Creative expression: AR and VR provide new tools for artists, designers, and creators to express their ideas in never-before-possible ways. Virtual art galleries, 3D sculptures, and interactive storytelling are just a few examples.

Increased accessibility: VR can bring experiences to people who might not otherwise have access to them. For example, students in remote areas can use VR to visit museums or landmarks, and people with disabilities can experience places and activities that might be difficult in the real world.

Challenges of AR and VR

Technical limitations: Creating realistic and responsive AR and VR experiences requires advanced technology, which can be expensive and challenging to develop. Additionally, VR systems need powerful computers to run smoothly, which can be costly.

Motion sickness: Some people experience motion sickness when using VR, as the brain can become confused by the difference between what the eyes see and what the body feels. This is a common challenge that developers are working to minimise.

Privacy concerns: AR systems that use cameras to capture the real world can raise privacy concerns, as they might inadvertently record and store images or videos of people without their consent.

Physical safety: Because VR users are immersed in a virtual world, they might not be aware of their physical surroundings, leading to accidents like bumping into furniture or tripping over objects.

Ethical issues: As AR and VR become more widespread, ethical questions arise about how these technologies should be used. For example, how should VR content be regulated to prevent misuse, and how can AR ensure it doesn't create a distorted view of reality?

9.6 Use of AR in daily life

Augmented Reality (AR) is a technology that blends the digital world with the real world. It allows us to see and interact with virtual objects as part of our surroundings. Here are some ways AR is used in our daily lives:

Education

AR makes learning more fun and interactive. For example, with AR, students can point their tablets at a picture of the solar system and see the planets come to life in 3D, helping them understand concepts better.

Shopping

AR helps people shop smarter. Some apps allow you to see how furniture or decorations will look in your home before you buy them. This means you can ensure something fits and looks good before purchasing.

Entertainment

Games like PokÈmon Go use AR to make the gaming experience more exciting. In these games, digital characters appear in the real world through your phone's camera, making it feel like you're catching Pokémon in your neighbourhood.

Navigation

AR can help with directions. Some navigation apps use AR to show arrows and signs on your phone screen that guide you to your destination, making it easier to follow directions.

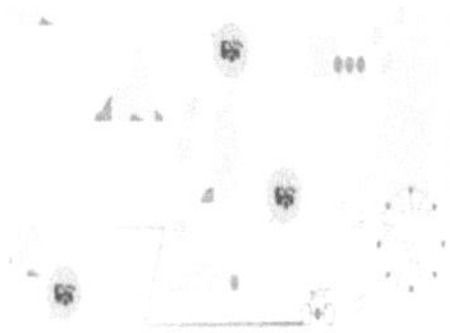

Social media

AR is used in social media apps to add fun effects to your photos and videos. Filters that add bunny ears or change your background are examples of AR at work.

9.7 Computer Vision

Computer Vision is a branch of Artificial Intelligence (AI) that enables machines to "see" and understand the visual world, just like humans do. It's like giving a computer eyes to recognise and interpret images, videos, and other visual information.

Imagine you take a picture of your pet dog. With computer vision, AI can analyse the picture and identify a dog, not a cat or a tree. This ability to recognise objects in images and videos makes computer vision so powerful.

Application of Computer Vision

Face Recognition

Face recognition technology unlocks smartphones and secures devices by recognising the user's face. The phone's camera captures an image of your face, and AI compares it to stored data to ensure it's you. This technology is also used in social media platforms to automatically tag friends in photos, making it easier to organise and share memories.

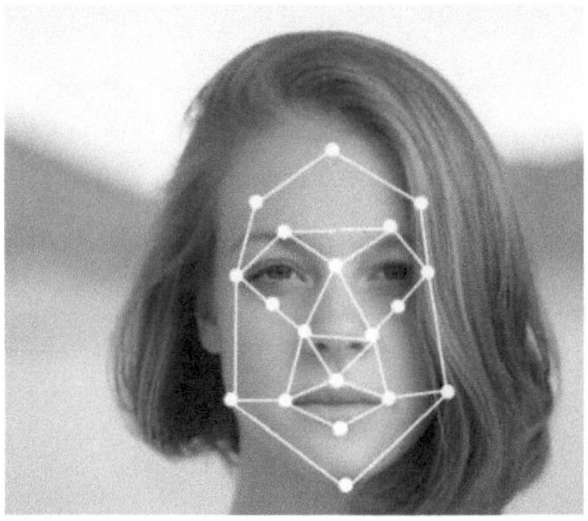

Healthcare

In healthcare, computer vision assists doctors in analyzing medical images like X-rays, MRIs, and CT scans. AI can identify patterns and abnormalities that might be challenging for the human eye to spot, such as early indicators of diseases like cancer. This technology supports quicker and more accurate diagnoses, enhancing patient care and outcomes.

Self-Driving cars

Computer vision is essential for self-driving cars, allowing them to "see" the road. The AI in these cars recognises traffic signs, pedestrians, other vehicles, and obstacles. It helps the car decide when to stop, turn, or slow down, ensuring a safe driving experience without human intervention.

9.8 Glossary

Augmented Reality (AR): Technology that overlays digital content onto the real world.
Virtual Reality (VR): Technology that creates fully immersive virtual environments.
Face Recognition: AI technology that identifies and verifies individuals by analysing facial features.
Image search: A feature that allows finding information or products online using images instead of text.

9.9 Summary

AR enhances the real world with digital elements, while VR creates immersive virtual environments.
AI focuses on learning and decision-making, while VR creates new digital experiences.
AR is used in education, shopping, and entertainment.
Computer Vision is an AI technology that enables machines to see and understand images with face recognition, image search, and healthcare applications.

Exercise

Exercise 1 – Choose the correct answer from the given options.
1. What does Augmented Reality (AR) do?
a) Creates a fully immersive digital environment
b) Enhances the real world with digital elements
c) Teaches computers to think like humans
d) Makes virtual worlds for gaming
2. Which of the following technologies requires a headset to use?
a) Augmented Reality
b) Virtual Reality
c) Face Recognition
d) Computer Vision

Exercise 2 – Check if the sentence is true or false.
1. Virtual Reality (VR) overlays digital elements onto the real world…..………..
2. Computer Vision helps AI recognise objects in images and videos…………..

Exercise 3 – Fill the blank space with the correct word.
1. ………………… Reality (VR) creates a fully immersive digital environment.
2. ……………. is used to recognise and identify individuals based on their facial features.

Exercise 4- Arrange the sentence in the correct sequence.
1. world / AR / elements / to / the / adds / digital / real.
2. used / to / images / Computer / Vision / analyze / is.

Exercise 5- Answer the following questions in your own words.
1. What is the main difference between AR and VR?
2. How does Computer Vision work in AI?

Answer

Exercise 1- 1. b) 2. b)
Exercise 2- 1. false 2. true
Exercise 3- 1. virtual 2. Face recognition
Exercise 4-
1. AR adds digital elements to the real world.
2. Computer Vision is used to analyze images.

Project

Create your own AR or VR experience.
To design a simple Augmented Reality (AR) or Virtual Reality (VR) experience using available tools or by creating a concept on paper.

Activity

Activity: AI-Powered art gallery
Objective:
To introduce students to the creative possibilities of AI by generating artwork using AI tools or their imagination and then showcasing their creations in a classroom gallery.

Activity: Create and curate an AI art gallery
1. Preparation:
• Provide students access to simple AI art generation tools (if available) or traditional art supplies like paper, markers, and coloured pencils.
• Explain how AI can create art by analysing patterns, generating designs, or enhancing creativity.

2. Instructions:
• AI-Generated Art (if tools are available): Students use an AI art tool to generate digital artwork. They can experiment with different styles, colours, and patterns to create something unique.
• AI-Inspired Traditional Art (if AI tools aren't available): Students create artwork inspired by what they imagine an AI might produce. They can think about how AI sees the world and use abstract patterns, futuristic designs, or unusual colour combinations.

3. Gallery setup:
• Once the artwork is complete, students help set up a classroom gallery. Each student displays their piece along with a short description of how AI inspired their work or how they used AI tools.
• The class can view and discuss the artwork through the gallery.

4. Gallery tour and discussion:
• As students tour the gallery, they take notes on their favourite pieces and think about how AI might influence art in the future.
• After the tour, have a group discussion about the experience. Questions could include: "How did AI change how you created art?" or "What surprised you about the artwork?"

5. Reflection:
• Students reflect on the role of AI in creativity and how it can be a tool for artists to explore new ideas and push the boundaries of traditional art forms.

Case Study

The Future Classroom: AR or VR?

Scenario:

A school is considering using new technologies to make learning more exciting. The principal decides whether to invest in Augmented Reality (AR) or Virtual Reality (VR) for classroom activities. AR would allow students to see digital models on their desks using tablets, like a 3D volcano or historical landmarks. VR would take students on virtual field trips to faraway places, such as ancient Rome or the bottom of the ocean, using VR headsets.

Challenge:

The school has a limited budget and can only choose one technology now. The principal asks the students to help make the decision by discussing the pros and cons of AR and VR for learning.

Group Discussion

The Impact of AR, VR, and AI on Our Future

The objective is to encourage students to think critically and collaboratively about the impact of AR, VR, and AI on the future. It helps students deepen their understanding, improve communication skills, explore ethical considerations, and foster teamwork as they discuss how these technologies can shape education, entertainment, daily life, etc.

Chapter-9
TEST PAPER
Augmented & Virtual Reality

Time Duration: 20 Minutes **Maximum Marks: 10**

General Instructions:
1. The question paper consists of 10 questions.
2. All questions are compulsory.

Choose the correct answer from the given options. **(1 X 2 = 2 marks)**

1. What does Virtual Reality (VR) primarily require to create an immersive experience?
a) Smartphone
b) VR Headset
c) Computer
d) Smartwatch
2. Which technology overlays digital information in the real world?
a) Artificial Intelligence (AI)
b) Virtual Reality (VR)
c) Augmented Reality (AR)
d) Computer Vision

Fill the blank space with the correct word. **(1 X 3 = 3 marks)**

1. Virtual Reality (VR) requires a ________ to immerse users in a __________ environment.
2. ________ Reality (AR) adds digital elements to the real world.

Answer the following questions in your own words. **(1 X 5 = 5 marks)**

1. What is the difference between Augmented Reality (AR) and Virtual Reality (VR)?
2. How does Computer Vision help AI systems?
3. In what ways is AI used in daily life?

Online Interactive Resources

Online Exam Paper:
Link: https://forms.gle/DossPHpapYXz1Nso7

QR Code:

Chapter 9 Videos Playlist:
Link: https://www.youtube.com/playlist?list=PLzlh_31VWEFrWrzVwPdZimCGwSnG-Iu5d

QR Code:

Annual Test Paper

Time Duration: 40 Minutes **Maximum Marks: 50**

General Instructions:

1. The paper comprises 25 questions divided into two sections: A and B.
2. All questions are compulsory.
3. Section A comprises filling in the blanks, stating true/false, one-word answers and choosing the correct answers for one mark each.
4. Section B comprises question numbers 1 to 5. These are short questions that carry two marks each.

SECTION-A

Fill in the Blanks **(1 X 10 = 10 marks)**

1. The two main types of computer memory are ________ and ________.
2. In Windows 11, the ________ feature helps users switch between open applications.
3. ________ is used to add images, sounds, or videos to a PowerPoint slide.
4. The ________ view in PowerPoint displays all slides as thumbnails.
5. The ________ key is used in combination with others to create shortcuts in Windows.
6. ________ is a unit of memory measurement that equals 1024 MB.
7. To create a new folder, you can use the ________ menu.
8. In Scratch, ________ are the characters or objects that perform actions.
9. The Internet is a global network that allows ________ of information.
10. ________ in AI refers to the ability of machines to make decisions.

True/False **(1 X 10 = 10 marks)**

1. RAM is permanent storage for data on a computer.
2. A presentation in PowerPoint can be saved with the extension .pptx.
3. The "Task View" feature is available in Windows 11.
4. A file and a folder are the same in Windows operating systems.
5. The "Insert" tab in PowerPoint is used to add new slides.
6. SmartArt can only be used in Microsoft Word.
7. Google Apps include tools like Gmail and Google Drive.
8. In Scratch, events are actions triggered by user interactions.
9. Artificial Intelligence can only be used in the field of robotics.
10. The desktop in Windows displays shortcuts and open files.

One Word **(1 X 10 = 10 marks)**

1. What is the primary memory in a computer called?
2. Name the global system of interconnected computer networks.
3. Which unit is larger: MB or GB?
4. What do we call the visual representation of information in PowerPoint?
5. What is the key combination to open the Start menu in Windows?
6. What type of files are created in PowerPoint?

7. What tool in Scratch helps make characters respond to key presses?
8. Which AI tool allows users to search for images or text on the web?
9. What feature in Windows 11 lets you view all running applications?
10. What is a single unit of data storage, often measured in bits?

Choose the Correct Option **(1 X 10 = 10 marks)**

1. Which of these is used to store data permanently?
a) RAM
b) ROM
c) CPU
d) Cache
2. In Windows, what allows you to quickly access commonly used files and applications?
a) Task View
b) Desktop
c) File Explorer
d) Shortcuts
3. Which of these applications is a part of Google Apps?
a) Excel
b) PowerPoint
c) Gmail
d) Outlook
4. What is the main purpose of SmartArt in PowerPoint?
a) To add sound
b) To organize visual information
c) To change slide layout
d) To save a presentation
5. Which memory is often referred to as temporary memory?
a) RAM
b) ROM
c) Hard Drive
d) Flash Drive
6. In PowerPoint, which view is used to see all slides at once?
a) Slide Show
b) Outline View
c) Slide Sorter
d) Notes View
7. Which Scratch block is used to start an action when the green flag is clicked?
a) Control Block
b) Event Block
c) Motion Block
d) Looks Block
8. What is the primary function of Task View in Windows 11?
a) To create new files
b) To view open apps
c) To edit documents
d) To open settings

9. What is a file extension commonly used for saving PowerPoint presentations?
a) .docx
b) .xlsx
c) .pptx
d) .txt
10. Artificial Intelligence that recognises speech is called:
a) Image Recognition
b) Speech Recognition
c) Language Processing
d) Data Mining

SECTION-B

Short Questions **(2 X 5 = 10 marks)**
1. Explain the difference between RAM and ROM in computer memory.
2. What is the purpose of creating folders on a computer, and how do they help in organising files?
3. Describe how to add and edit SmartArt in a PowerPoint slide.
4. Explain the role of Task View in Windows 11.
5. What is the importance of Artificial Intelligence in today's technology?

Online Interactive Resources

Online Exam Paper:
Link: https://forms.gle/oyTUdGuGUHCczPHm6

QR Code:

ADDITIONAL RESOURCE

Computer Class 4 Book Playlist:
Link:
https://www.youtube.com/playlist?list=PLzlh_31VWEFo3CtWjiAWaCGupAYW2hXt

QR Code:

Computer Class 5 Book Playlist:
Link: https://www.youtube.com/playlist?list=PLzlh_31VWEFr6EeSh8t97XPPQMIXlv6iQ

QR Code:

NEP Video:
Link: https://youtu.be/6sKTXOY_yFw

QR Code:

Credit Score Video:
Link: https://youtu.be/NxMHHIt9PcI

QR Code:

CBSE Video Playlist:
Link: https://youtu.be/uOkCDapmhKc

QR Code: